Little FOLK

COLORING BOOK

Christine Karron

LITTLE FOLK
COLORING BOOK

This printing 2026
Copyright © 2025 Christine Karron

Published by Blue Angel Publishing®
10 Trafford Court, Wheelers Hill
Victoria, Australia 3150

info@blueangelonline.com
blueangelonline.com

By Christine Karron

Edited by Cherise Asmah

Designed by Gemma Christensen

Blue Angel Publishing is a registered trademark of Blue Angel Gallery Pty. Ltd.

ISBN: 978-1-922574-41-1

Printed on sustainably sourced paper, with soy-based inks.

The coloring frenzy continues! I am very excited to present you the *Little Folk* coloring book!

This is the third book in my special collection coloring book series. Included in this coloring book are 50 of my most popular and favourite illustrations, as well as four additional, exclusive new designs, *Crowned in Snowflakes, May Bells, Ms. Pumpkin* and *Rosehip Elfling.*

As an artist with a huge imagination, I like to fantasize about hidden places in fairytale forests, meadows and lakes, with dwellings of ethereal beings I so much love to create. These quirky and cute little personalities pop up in my head and want me to draw them on paper.

I hope you enjoy bringing all these whimsical elves, fairies and other fantastical characters in this book to life through coloring as much as I do.

Christine Karron

AUTUMN ENCOUNTERS

AUTUMN FOREST WITCH

BEST FROGGY FRIEND

BIRD BATH

COOKIE ELVES

COWGIRL MERMAID

CROWNED IN SNOWFLAKES

DEW DROPLET

DRAGONLING

ELFLING'S SHELTER

FAIRY BOOK

FAIRY DUST

FAIRY FLOWER CROWN

FAIRY GIRL WITH BIRDS

FAIRY GODMOTHER

FAIRY HEART

FAIRY WITH LIZARD

FAUN JINGLE

FLOWER GIRL

FLOWERLING

GARDEN FRIENDS

GOOD MORNING FAIRY

HAPPY FAIRY

HELPING HANDS

HEN HOUSE GOSSIP

JESTER

LEAF RIDER

LITTLE FAIRY BOY

LITTLE FAIRY MONSTER

LUCKY CLOVER

MAY BELLS

MERMAID'S SHOES

MS. LEPRECHAUN

MS. PUMPKIN

MUSHROOM MOOD

PEA ELFLING

PIRATE

RACOON RASCALS

ROSEHIP ELFLING

SCRATCHY SWEATER

S E E D L I N G

SLEEPING BEAUTY

SNAIL ELFLING

SPRING BRINGER

STAR CATCHER

SUMMER NIGHT FIDDLER

SUMMER RAIN

SWEET MAPLE

THE FROG PRINCE

TROLL GIRL AND FOX SERENADE

TROLLERINA

UNICORN PRINCESS

WHIMSY FAIRY CELISE

WINTER WARMTH

BLUE ANGEL®
PUBLISHING

For more information on this or
any Blue Angel Publishing® release,
please visit our website at:

www.blueangelonline.com